Butter y
and m >

INTRODUCTION

Butterflies are among our most familiar and much-loved insects. With nearly 60 different species in the UK, they come in a wonderful variety of colours and patterns. Moths have much to offer too. With over 2,500 species to discover in the UK, they are every bit as beautiful and they have some pretty crazy caterpillars too.

The next time you are in your garden or out and about, take your i-SPY book with you and see what you can spot. Butterflies like to fly when it is warm and still so choose a sunny day in the spring or summer with very little wind to go out looking for them.

Some of the species of moth featured in this book are day-flying, but some only come out at night so to see them requires some detective work! Many night-flying moths are attracted to light so you could hang up a white sheet with a bright torch shining on it, or look around the outdoor lights near your home, such as a porch or garage light. In the daytime you might spot them resting on fences, walls or vegetation.

Many moth and butterfly caterpillars can be found during the daytime, most commonly from May to September. You can also try looking in your garden with a torch on mild winter nights, when some moth caterpillars come out to feed. It is best to avoid touching hairy caterpillars as some have hairs that can irritate your skin. Always be gentle when handling any wildlife and always make sure you wash your hands afterwards.

To discover more about butterflies, moths and caterpillars you can visit www.butterfly-conservation.org or www.munchingcaterpillars.org.

How to use your i-SPY book

As you work through this book, you will notice that the entries are arranged in four main groupings. These are caterpillars, butterflies, moths, or the signs that these creatures have been around. You need 1000 points to send off for your i-SPY certificate (see page 64) but that is not too difficult because there are masses of points in every book. Each entry has a star or circle and points value beside it. The stars represent harder to spot entries. As you make each i-SPY, write your score in the circle or star.

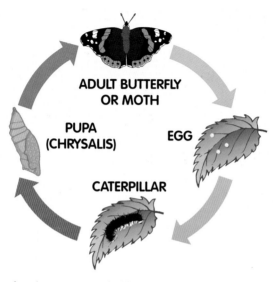

There are four distinct stages to the life cycle of a butterfly or moth. It starts when a female lays her eggs. Most of the time she will do this on or near a plant that her caterpillars like to eat so that once they have hatched they have a food source waiting for them. The caterpillars spend most of their time eating and growing. While the caterpillar grows, it sheds its skin 4 or 5 times until finally it finds a safe place and its last skin turns into a harder surface called a pupa, or chrysalis. Inside this shell the caterpillar goes through a process called metamorphosis, where it completely changes its shape. The change from caterpillar to adult butterfly or moth may take from just a few days to many months depending on the species. The adult butterfly or moth finally emerges by splitting the skin of the pupa and crawling out. At first they are damp and wrinkled, but they pump fluid into their wings until they are dry and strong enough to fly. They feed on nectar from flowers to give them energy as they begin their search for a mate.

LARGE WHITE

Points: 5

Unpopular with gardeners, these caterpillars can easily be found munching on cabbages, brussel sprouts and other brassicas.

 Points: 5

PEACOCK

The black, spiky caterpillars of the Peacock butterfly can be found feeding on nettles in early summer.

PALE TUSSOCK

Points: 25

These funky looking caterpillars are a bright greenish-yellow, with four tufts of golden yellow hairs. They grow slowly between late June and early October, then overwinter as pupae.

CINNABAR

Points: 5

These striking black and yellow striped caterpillars feed on ragwort from July to September. Often a single plant can be seen covered in caterpillars.

Points: 10

MULLEIN

Often spotted in gardens, these caterpillars feed on various species of mullein. They are more easily seen in the caterpillar stage, as the brown coloured adults are well camouflaged against dead leaves and stalks.

GARDEN TIGER

Points: 15

These caterpillars are affectionately known as 'woolly bears' referring to the dense furry hair that covers their body.

Points: 25

PUSS MOTH

This bizarre looking caterpillar feeds on aspen, poplar and willow. When disturbed, it rears its head and waves the twin tails on its rear end.

7

Points: 20

ELEPHANT HAWK-MOTH

This caterpillar feeds mostly on rosebay willowherb and fuchsia and gets its name from its resemblance to an elephant's trunk.

Points: 25

DRINKER

Fully grown, these caterpillars are up to 7 cm in length. In winter they can sometimes be found at rest on grass stems and on the twigs of bushes. In the spring they feed mainly at night, but during the day can be found resting low down on vegetation.

BUFF-TIP

Points: 15

These yellow and black caterpillars feed on deciduous trees, mainly oaks, birch and hazel. They can be seen from July to early October.

COMMA

Points: 5

This beautiful orange butterfly has a very distinctive shape as the wings have wavy edges. It has a white comma on the underside of its wings.

SMALL TORTOISESHELL

Points: 5

The Small Tortoiseshell is one of our most widespread butterfly species. It hibernates in the UK and can be seen from early spring to autumn, making it a popular garden visitor.

PEACOCK

Points: 5

The Peacock is one of our most recognisable butterflies with red wings and bright eyespots to scare off predators. The undersides of the wings are very dark and look like dead leaves.

PAINTED LADY

Points: 5

The Painted Lady is a migrant that flies all the way from Europe and North Africa. In some years it is an abundant butterfly, frequenting gardens and other flowery places in late summer.

RED ADMIRAL

Points: 5

The big, bold and beautiful Red Admiral is a common sight in summer gardens. It can survive over winter as an adult, usually in sheds or garages.

Points: 20

WHITE ADMIRAL

This is a spectacular woodland butterfly, with white-banded black wings and a distinctive delicate flight. It can be found in the south of England.

PURPLE EMPEROR

Points: 40

This magnificent butterfly flies high in the tree-tops of woodlands in central-southern England. It is large and dark with white-banded wings. The males have a purple sheen.

ORANGE-TIP

Points: 5

Only the males have the bright orange wing tips, but both the male and female have a mottled grey-green underwing that can help distinguish this species from the Small White and Green-veined White.

 Points: 5

BRIMSTONE

The delicate yellow Brimstone looks just like a leaf when its wings are folded together! It rests in this position to avoid being seen by birds that want to eat it.

GREEN-VEINED WHITE

Points: 5

The wings of this widespread and common butterfly are white, with prominent greenish veins on the hind wing. The upper wings have one or more spots.

Points: 5

LARGE WHITE

The dark black wing tips distinguish this butterfly from its smaller cousin the Small White. Only the females have these spots on the wings

SMALL WHITE

Points: 5

The black markings on the wings are not as dark as they are on the Large White, but these butterflies can be confused with female Orange-tips when the wings are open.

WOOD WHITE

Points: 40

This small and dainty white butterfly has declined rapidly over the past few decades. Males fly almost continuously throughout the day in fine weather, patrolling to find a mate.

MARBLED WHITE

Points: 20

The black and white checked wings of the Marbled White make it unlikely to be mistaken for another butterfly. It is found in flowery grassland but may stray into gardens.

 Points: 30

LARGE HEATH

The Large Heath is restricted to wet, boggy habitats. The adults always sit with their wings closed and can fly even in quite dull weather.

SMALL HEATH

Points: 20

The Small Heath is a small and easily overlooked butterfly that flies only in sunshine and rarely settles more than a metre above the ground. Its wings are always kept closed when at rest.

Points: 10

If you look closely, you can see that the Ringlet has small circles on the underwing which give it its name. Bramble and Wild Privet flowers are favourite nectar sources, and adults continue to fly with a characteristic bobbing flight in dull, cloudy conditions when most other butterflies are inactive.

GATEKEEPER

Points: 10

The Gatekeeper gets its name because it likes to live in hedgerows, so it can often be spotted around gates.

Points: 5

MEADOW BROWN

The Meadow Brown is one of the most common and widespread butterflies in the UK. It is another species that prefers grassland.

SCOTCH ARGUS

Points: 20

As its name suggests, this butterfly is found predominantly in Scotland where it flies in tall, damp grassland.

Points: 20

WALL

This orange and brown butterfly often basks on walls, stones and bare ground.

SPECKLED WOOD

Points: 10

Dark brown with creamy white patches on its wings, the aptly named Speckled Wood flies in partially shaded woodland with dappled sunlight.

Points: 20

ADONIS BLUE

This beautiful butterfly has distinctive black lines that cross the white edges of the wings. The males are a brilliant blue while the females are chocolate brown.

LARGE BLUE

Top Spot!   Points: 50

This is the largest and rarest of our blue butterflies, distinguished by the unmistakable row of black spots on its upper forewing. The Large Blue has always been rare in the UK and became extinct in 1979, but it has been reintroduced from continental Europe to southwest England as part of a highly successful conservation project.

SMALL BLUE

Points: 20

Our smallest resident butterfly is easily overlooked, partly because of its size and dusky colouring, but partly because it is often confined to small patches of sheltered grassland.

Points: 25

SILVER-STUDDED BLUE

A rare butterfly confined to small colonies in southern England and Wales. The males have upperwings that are blue with a dark border. Females are brown with a row of red spots.

COMMON BLUE

Points: 5

The Common Blue is the most widespread blue butterfly in the UK and Ireland. The male has blue wings with a black-brown border and a thin white fringe. The female is brown with a blue dusting near its body and fewer orange spots along the lower edges of its wings.

Points: 10

HOLLY BLUE

Often found in parks and gardens, the Holly Blue emerges early in the spring and congregates around holly, on which it lays its eggs.

CHALK HILL BLUE

Points: 10

This butterfly is confined to chalk and limestone grassland in southern England and numbers have declined in recent decades. The males have milky blue upperwings, with a thin black-brown border and a thin white fringe. The females have darkish brown upperwings, with orange spots around the edges of the wings and a dusting of blue near the body.

Points: 25

BROWN ARGUS

The Brown Argus has dark brown wings fringed in white, with a row of orange spots along the outer edges of the wings. The wings have a blue sheen at certain angles.

SILVER-SPOTTED SKIPPER

Points: 30

A small butterfly with a low darting flight, the Silver-spotted Skipper has lots of silvery spots on the underside of the hindwings. It is found in southern England.

GRIZZLED SKIPPER

Points: 30

This small, springtime butterfly has a striking black and white appearance. It is found throughout England and Wales but is becoming increasingly rare.

Points: 25

DINGY SKIPPER

This small, brown and grey butterfly is found across the UK but is becoming increasingly rare.

LARGE SKIPPER

Points: 10 (10)

Large Skippers may be seen feeding on flowers, bramble being a favourite. Males are most often found perching in a sunny position, waiting for passing females.

(10) **Points: 10**

SMALL SKIPPER

Small Skippers are marvellous flyers, darting through tall grass stems. They have bright, orange-brown wings with the forewings angled above the hindwings.

WHITE-LETTER HAIRSTREAK

Points: 30

This small butterfly lives among the tops of elm trees throughout England and Wales. The underwings are brown, with a white W-shaped streak, an orange edge and small tails.

 Points: 50   **Top Spot!**

BLACK HAIRSTREAK

The Black Hairstreak is one of our rarest and most elusive butterflies, staying in the tree canopy, feeding on honeydew from aphids and spending little time in flight. It is restricted to the East Midlands.

GREEN HAIRSTREAK

Points: 20

The only green-coloured butterfly in the UK, although the metallic green colouring is only on the undersides of the wings.

Points: 25

PURPLE HAIRSTREAK

This handsome butterfly is widely distributed in England and Wales wherever there are oak trees; even a solitary tree may support a colony. Males have a purple sheen, females (like this one), have a purple mark on the forewing.

BROWN HAIRSTREAK

Points: 40

The largest hairstreak in the UK is an elusive butterfly that spends most of its time either high in the canopy of trees, or hiding in hedgerows.

GLANVILLE FRITILLARY

Points: 40

The Glanville Fritillary is named after Lady Eleanor Glanville, who first found the butterfly in England in the 1690s. This butterfly is only active in bright sunshine and can be hard to track with its rapid wingbeats and gliding style of flight. It is found only on the Isle of Wight.

HIGH BROWN FRITILLARY

Top Spot! Points: 50

This large, powerful butterfly is usually seen flying swiftly over the tops of bracken or low vegetation in woodland clearings. Once widespread in England and Wales, it has undergone a dramatic decline since the 1950s and is now reduced to under 40 sites where conservationists are working to save it from extinction.

Points: 20

DARK GREEN FRITILLARY

This large, powerful, orange and black butterfly is one of our most widespread fritillaries and can be seen flying rapidly in a range of open, sunny habitats.

SILVER-WASHED FRITILLARY

Points: 25

The swooping flight of this large and graceful butterfly is one of the most beautiful sights to be found in woodland during high summer. A large fast flying butterfly, separated from other fritillaries by its pointed wings and silver streaks on the undersides.

Points: 40

MARSH FRITILLARY

The checked wings of this lovely butterfly are more colourful and brightly patterned than any of our other fritillaries. The Marsh Fritillary is threatened, not only in the UK but across Europe, and is therefore the focus of much conservation effort.

PEARL-BORDERED FRITILLARY

Points: 40

This is one of the earliest fritillaries to emerge and can be found as early as April in woodland clearings or rough hillsides with bracken. It was once very widespread but has rapidly declined in recent decades.

Points: 30 **SMALL PEARL-BORDERED FRITILLARY**

This butterfly remains widespread in Scotland and Wales, but has undergone a severe decline in England. It is similar in size to the Pearl-bordered Fritillary but can be identified from the more numerous whitish pearls on the underside hind wings.

DUKE OF BURGUNDY

Points: 40

The Duke of Burgundy is a small, springtime butterfly that frequents scrubby grassland and sunny woodland clearings.

Points: 15

SMALL COPPER

This butterfly may be small, but it is perfectly formed! The beautiful orange wings with tiny black spots really stand out on a sunny day.

SWALLOWTAIL

Top Spot!   Points: 50

Found only in the Norfolk Broads, this is one of our rarest and most spectacular butterflies. They are a large and strong-flying butterfly with a distinctive tail on the hindwings.

37

CURRANT CLEARWING

Points: 10

This day-flying moth is said to mimic wasps or hornets for protection from predators. It can be seen in gardens, allotments and fruit fields. Often found near currant bushes.

JERSEY TIGER

Points: 30

This moth was once restricted to the Channel Islands but is now found all along the south coast of England and its range is expanding northwards. It flies during the day and at night from July to September.

SCARLET TIGER

Points: 10

This tropical-looking moth is very distinctive. It frequently flies in the sunshine, or can be found resting on leaves. Spot them in June and July.

 Points: 15

CHIMNEY SWEEPER

A small, sooty black moth with white fringes on its wing tips. This moth is active by day, especially in sunshine.

MOTHER SHIPTON

Points: 15

Found in a range of open, grassy habitats, this moth is brown with a pale pattern on the forewing, said to resemble a witch's face. It flies by day.

EMPEROR MOTH

Points: 25

Males fly rapidly in the day and are often mistaken for a Small Tortoiseshell butterfly. The female is larger than the male with slightly different markings, has a paler colour and does not have the feathered antennae of the male.

RUBY TIGER

Points: 10

The English name of this moth is most appropriate for those found in southern England. In northern England and Ireland, the forewings are darker with some blackish tints on the hindwings.

Points: 10

OAK EGGAR

A large moth, the male is a darker brown with a yellow line on the wings and feathery antennae. Both males and females have a white spot on the forewing. Males fly by day in a zig-zag fashion, particularly in afternoon sunshine.

CINNABAR

Points: 5

This distinctive moth is fairly common and can often be seen in the daytime from May to July.

Points: 5

SILVER Y

Named after the pale, Y-shaped markings on the wings, this moth is common and can be seen during the day as well as at night. It migrates to the UK from Europe and North Africa.

SIX-SPOT BURNET

Points: 5

With six bright red spots against glossy black, this moth is easily spotted flying slowly from flower to flower in bright sunshine.

HUMMINGBIRD HAWK-MOTH

Points: 15

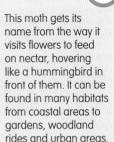

This moth gets its name from the way it visits flowers to feed on nectar, hovering like a hummingbird in front of them. It can be found in many habitats from coastal areas to gardens, woodland rides and urban areas.

Points: 20

ELEPHANT HAWK-MOTH

This is one of our most beautiful and recognisable moths with its pink and green colouring. It is the caterpillar that gives it its name, due to its resemblance to an elephant's trunk.

POPLAR HAWK-MOTH

Points: 15

This is probably our commonest hawk-moth and has a distinctive shape when at rest, holding its hind wings forward of its front wings. This breaks up the triangular shape of the moth that some predators recognise.

Points: 20

LIME HAWK-MOTH

The wing shape, markings and pink and green colour are unlike those of any other hawk-moth found in the UK. Adults can be seen between May and early July.

Points: 50   Top Spot!   **PRIVET HAWK-MOTH**

This magnificent moth is our largest resident hawk-moth with a wingspan of between 9 and 12 cm. It has a pink and black striped abdomen and hindwings.

It is usually found in woodland and gardens where it likes to feed on nectar from highly scented flowers.

EYED HAWK-MOTH

Points: 20

This is a well camouflaged moth when resting, but if it is disturbed it will flash its hindwings which are marked with striking blue and pink "eyes" to scare predators away.

Points: 15

ANGLE SHADES

This pretty moth is found in virtually all habitats and can frequently be seen during the day resting on walls, fences and vegetation.

Points: 20

FOX MOTH

This moth is named after its colouration; males are usually a foxy-red/brown and the larger females are grey-brown. Spot them in May and June.

ARGENT & SABLE

Points: 40

This day-flying moth has distinctive black and white markings. It has suffered huge declines in England and Wales and is in need of urgent conservation action.

Points: 20

RED UNDERWING

This large moth has a wingspan of between 6 and 8 cm. The red hindwing, which gives it the English name, has a black band around the scalloped margin, fringed with white.

BRIMSTONE

Points: 10

This common and vibrantly coloured yellow moth can frequently be seen flying just before dusk.

Points: 20

CHINESE CHARACTER

This unmistakeable moth uses visual mimicry to avoid being eaten. When at rest, the wings are held steeply over the body, and combined with a white, brown and grey wing pattern, it closely resembles a bird dropping!

SWALLOW-TAILED MOTH

Points: 25

Another vividly coloured species with a pointed tail on the hindwings each with two small dark brown spots. They are occasionally disturbed during the day but are otherwise strictly nocturnal.

COMMON FOOTMAN

Points: 15

When at rest, the wings are gently curled flat over the body. They can sometimes be seen basking in the sunshine on tree trunks, walls or posts.

BURNISHED BRASS

Points: 20

This unmistakeable moth has a spectacular brassy, metallic sheen on the forewings. The adults feed at dusk at the flowers of honeysuckle, buddleia and Red Valerian.

GARDEN TIGER

Points: 15

If disturbed, this moth displays its orange hindwings with blue-black spots and can produce a clear yellow fluid from two ducts just behind the head. Both are warnings to predators that they are not good to eat!

Points: 20

VAPOURER

The male of this species has broad orange-brown wings with a pair of white eye spots. They fly in sunshine and are rarely seen at rest. The nearly wingless female has a plump grey-brown body.

BUFF ERMINE

Points: 10

This is a pretty moth that looks very furry. It flies from May to July and will often visit outdoor lights.

BUFF-TIP

Points: 20

You will need sharp eyes to spot this wonderful moth. It looks very much like a broken birch twig when found at rest on vegetation during the day. They can be spotted late May to July.

Points: 25

BLOOD-VEIN

This moth has buff-coloured wings with a distinctive pink or brownish-red line across the fore and hindwings. They can occasionally be seen during the day around low vegetation.

FORESTER

Points: 40

The Forester flies by day in sunshine from mid-May to July. It likes damp meadows and coastal marshes. It is declining, and in need of special conservation action.

Points: 10

MAGPIE

This pretty speckled moth flies in July and August and is quite common in the UK, although it is declining in many areas.

LIGHT EMERALD

Points: 10

These beautiful pale green moths may often be disturbed from rest where they sit on the underside of trees and shrubs. Spot them from late May through to September.

DEATH'S-HEAD HAWK-MOTH

Top Spot!   Points: 50

With a whopping wingspan of 8-12 cm, this is the largest moth to be found in the UK. It is named after the skull-like marking on its thorax. This immigrant from southern Europe can be seen in the UK from early May to late November, though most commonly from late August to late October.

CHRYSALIS

Points: 30

When they have eaten enough, caterpillars will pupate. Butterflies form a chrysalis, often attached to the caterpillar foodplant, or at the base of the plant. The change from caterpillar to adult butterfly or moth may take from just a few days to many months depending on the species.

Points: 30

PUPAE

Moth pupae are often dark brown and lie buried in the soil, so you may come across them while digging in the garden.

COCOON

Points: 30

A cocoon is an extra protective layer that some moths form around their pupa. They are often attached to stems of plants, or found underground.

Points: 5

NIBBLED LEAF

Caterpillars are eating machines! Look out for tell-tale nibbled leaves or bare stems on trees or shrubs.

FRASS

Points: 30

Caterpillars produce a lot of poo! The droppings are known as 'frass' and are often very small, dark pellets which you might spot on or under nibbled vegetation.

EGGS

Points: 20

Butterflies and moths lay very small eggs, sometimes in clusters and sometimes on their own. They are usually laid on the leaves of plants that the caterpillars like to eat.

You don't have to travel far to see butterflies and moths. Our parks, gardens and outdoor spaces can all be great places to spot common species. There might be colourful Red Admirals and Peacocks feasting on your back garden buddleia bush and the grassy bits of your local park might just be home to Meadow Browns and Ringlets.

Sadly, our butterflies and moths are in trouble. Many species like the Small Tortoiseshell have seen their numbers tumble in recent years. But you can help scientists discover the best ways to protect butterflies and moths in the future by counting how many you see during the summer.

The Big Butterfly Count, run by wildlife charity Butterfly Conservation, is the world's largest butterfly survey. The Count takes place every year with participants spending 15 minutes counting butterflies.

All you need to do is to download a free butterfly ID sheet or app at the bigbutterflycount.org website and go outside and start counting. It's best to count on a sunny day when butterflies are more active and easier to spot. When you've finished your Count you can send in your sightings using the Big Butterfly Count website or app.

Butterflies are useful species to spot as they react very quickly to changes in the places that they live. If butterflies are struggling they can give scientists an early warning that there are problems in the environment and that other wildlife might also be in trouble.
The Count lets scientists find out how different species of butterfly are coping, which then lets them plan conservation work that can help these butterflies in the future.

The Big Butterfly Count includes 18 species of widespread butterfly and two species of common moths that fly in the daytime.

The Count takes place for three weeks in July and August.

For full details visit
www.bigbutterflycount.org

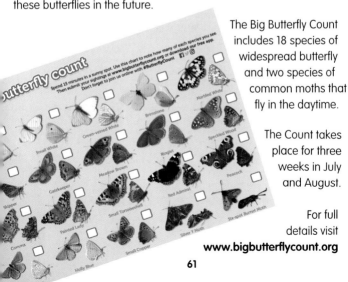

INDEX

Adonis Blue 21
Angle Shades 46
Argent and Sable 47
Big Butterfly Count 60
Black Hairstreak 29
Blood-vein 52
Brimstone (Butterfly) 14
Brimstone (Moth) 48
Brown Argus 25
Brown Hairstreak 31
Buff Ermine 51
Buff-tip 52
Buff-tip (Caterpillar) 9
Burnished Brass 50
Chalk Hill Blue 25
Chimney Sweeper 39
Chinese Character 48
chrysalis 56
Cinnabar 42
Cinnabar (Caterpillar) 6
cocoon 57
Comma 10
Common Blue 24
Common Footman 50
Currant Clearwing 38
Dark Green Fritillary 33
Death's-head Hawk-
    moth 55
Dingy Skipper 27
Drinker (Caterpillar) 9
Duke of Burgundy 36
eggs 59
Elephant Hawk-moth
    43
Elephant Hawk-moth
    (Caterpillar) 8
Emperor Moth 40
Eyed Hawk-moth 46
Forester 53

Fox Moth 47
frass 58
Garden Tiger 51
Garden Tiger
    (Caterpillar) 6
Gatekeeper 19
Glanville Fritillary 32
Green Hairstreak 30
Green-veined White 15
Grizzled Skipper 27
High Brown Fritillary 33
Holly Blue 24
Hummingbird Hawk-
    moth 43
Jersey Tiger 38
Large Blue 22
Large Heath 17
Large Skipper 28
Large White 15
Large White
    (Caterpillar) 4
Light Emerald 54
Lime Hawk-moth 44
Magpie 54
Marbled White 17
Marsh Fritillary 34
Meadow Brown 19
Mother Shipton 39
Mullein (Caterpillar) 6
nibbled leaf 58
Oak Eggar 41
Orange-tip 14
Painted Lady 11
Pale Tussock
    (Caterpillar) 5
Peacock 11
Peacock (Caterpillar) 4
Pearl-bordered
    Fritillary 34

Poplar Hawk-moth 44
Privet Hawk-moth 45
pupae 56
Purple Emperor 13
Purple Hairstreak 30
Puss Moth
    (Caterpillar) 7
Red Admiral 12
Red Underwing 48
Ringlet 19
Ruby Tiger 41
Scarlet Tiger 39
Scotch Argus 20
Silver-spotted
    Skipper 26
Silver-studded Blue 23
Silver-washed
    Fritillary 33
Silver Y 42
Six-spot Burnet 42
Small Blue 23
Small Copper 36
Small Heath 18
Small Pearl-bordered
    Fritillary 35
Small Skipper 28
Small Tortoiseshell 10
Small White 15
Speckled Wood 21
Swallowtail 37
Swallow-tailed Moth 49
Vapourer 51
Wall 20
White Admiral 12
White-letter
    Hairstreak 29
Wood White 16

ACKNOWLEDGEMENTS

The publishers would like to thank all those involved in the creation of this i-SPY book. In particular we would like to thank everyone at **Butterfly Conservation** (butterfly-conservation.org) who provided the expert insight, photographs and descriptions. Individual photographers are listed below.

PHOTO CREDITS

Title Page: Colin Robert Varndell/Shutterstock
Intro Page: Domnitsky/Shutterstock
4: Peacock (Caterpillar), Kelly Thomas
4: Large White (Caterpillar), David Green
5: Pale Tussock (Caterpillar), Patrick Clement
5: Garden Tiger (Caterpillar), David Green
6: Cinnabar (Caterpillar), James Peat
6: Mullein (Caterpillar), Patrick Clement
7: Puss Moth (Caterpillar), John Bebbington
7: Elephant Hawk-moth (Caterpillar), John Bebbington
8: Buff-tip (Caterpillar), Bob Eade
9: Drinker (Caterpillar), Bob Eade
10: Comma, Matt Berry
10: Small Tortoiseshell, Bob Eade
11: Painted Lady, Iain H Leach
11: Peacock (Butterfly), Neil Hulme
12: Red Admiral, Iain H Leach
12: White Admiral, Iain H Leach
13: Purple Emperor, Iain H Leach
14: Brimstone (Butterfly), Iain H Leach
14: Orange-tip, Iain H Leach
15: Green-veined White, Iain H Leach
15: Large White, Steve Maskell
15: Small White, Tim Melling
16: Wood White, Mike McKenzie
16: Large Heath, Iain H Leach
17: Marbled White, Bob Eade
18: Small Heath, Tim Melling
19: Gatekeeper, Mark Searle
19: Meadow Brown, Mark Searle
19: Ringlet, Neil Hulme
20: Scotch Argus, Tim Melling
20: Wall, Iain H Leach
21: Adonis Blue, Iain H Leach
21: Speckled Wood, Peter Eeles
22: Large Blue, Keith Warmington

23: Small Blue, Mark Searle
23: Silver-studded Blue, Tony Cox
24: Common Blue, Keith Warmington
24: Holly Blue, Iain H Leach
25: Brown Argus, Bob Eade
25: Chalk Hill Blue, Iain H Leach
26: Silver-spotted Skipper, Neil Hulme
27: Dingy Skipper, Iain H Leach
27: Grizzled Skipper, Iain H Leach
28: Large Skipper, Steve Maskell
28: Small Skipper, Iain H Leach
29: Black Hairstreak, Iain H Leach
29: White-letter Hairstreak, Iain H Leach
30: Green Hairstreak, Iain H Leach
30: Purple Hairstreak, Tim Melling
31: Brown Hairstreak, Iain H Leach
32: Glanville Fritillary, Mark Searle
33: Dark Green Fritillary, Heath McDonald
33: High Brown Fritillary, Iain H Leach
33: Silver-washed Fritillary, Iain H Leach
34: Marsh Fritillary, Iain H Leach
34: Pearl-bordered Fritillary, Mark Searle
35: Small Pearl-bordered Fritillary, Mark Searle
36: Small Copper, Bob Eade
36: Duke of Burgundy, Bob Eade
37: Swallowtail, Iain H Leach
38: Currant Clearwing, Iain H Leach
38: Jersey Tiger, Mark Parsons
39: Chimney Sweeper, Patrick Clement
39: Mother Shipton, Patrick Clement
39: Scarlet Tiger, Chris Manley
40: Emperor Moth, Iain H Leach
40: Oak Eggar, Garry Barlow
41: Ruby Tiger, Iain H Leach
42: Cinnabar, Mark Parsons
42: Silver Y, Mark Parsons

42: Six-spot Burnet, Patrick Clement
43: Elephant Hawk-moth, Shane Farrell
43: Hummingbird Hawk-moth, David Green
44: Lime Hawk-moth, Keith Warmington
44: Poplar Hawk-moth, Keith Warmington
45: Privet Hawk-moth, Keith Warmington
46: Eyed Hawk-moth, Mark Parsons
46: Angle Shades, Iain H Leach
47: Argent & Sable, Garry Barlow
47: Fox Moth, Iain H Leach
48: Brimstone (Moth), Robert Thompson
48: Chinese Character, Rob Skinner
48: Red Underwing, David Green
49: Swallow-tailed Moth, Robert Thompson
50: Burnished Brass, Iain H Leach
50: Common Footman, Robert Thompson
51: Buff Ermine, David Green
51: Garden Tiger, Shane Farrell
51: Vapourer, Patrick Clement
52: Blood-vein, Les Evans-Hill
52: Buff-tip, David Green
53: Forester, Iain H Leach
54: Light Emerald, David Green
54: Magpie, Robert Thompson
55: Death's-head Hawk-moth, Les Evans-Hill
56: chrysalis, Peter Eeles
56: pupae, Roy Leverton
57: cocoon, Patrick Clement
58: frass, John Bebbington
59: nibbled leaf, Jim Asher
59: eggs, Peter Eeles
60: Peacock (Butterfly), Maureen Rush
60: Child with Green-veined White, K Cruickshanks
64: Orange-tip chrysalis, David Morley

i-SPY

How to get your i-SPY certificate and badge

Let us know when you've become a super-spotter with 1000 points and we'll send you a special certificate and badge!

HERE'S WHAT TO DO!

- ✓ Ask an adult to check your score.

- ✓ Visit www.collins.co.uk/i-SPY to apply for your certificate. If you are under the age of 13 you will need a parent or guardian to do this.

- ✓ We'll send your certificate via email and you'll receive a brilliant badge through the post!